Which Seeds Will Grow?

poems

Andrew J. Calis

IRON
PEN

PARACLETE PRESS
BREWSTER, MASSACHUSETTS

For Stephanie

and for Aaron, Lily, Siena, and Jude

2024 First Printing

Which Seeds Will Grow: poems

978-1-64060-953-2

Copyright © 2024 by Andrew J. Calis

The poem excerpt on page 71 is from "A Poet and a Shrink (III)" in *Yours, Purple Gallinule*; © 2022 by Ewa Chrusciel. The quote appears with the permission of Omnidawn Publishing. All rights reserved.

The Iron Pen name and logo are trademarks of Paraclete Press.

   Library of Congress Cataloging-in-Publication Data
Names: Calis, Andrew J., 1987- author.
Title: Which seeds will grow? : poems / Andrew J. Calis.
Description: Brewster, Massachusetts : Paraclete Press, 2024. | Summary:
   "Calis's profound poetry has the intensity of Hopkins, while layering
   light on light in the hope of helping us to see"-- Provided by
   publisher.
Identifiers: LCCN 2024018614 (print) | LCCN 2024018615 (ebook) |
ISBN 9781640609532 (trade paperback) | ISBN 9781640609549 (epub)
Subjects: BISAC: POETRY / Subjects & Themes / Inspirational & Religious |
   POETRY / Subjects & Themes / Places | LCGFT: Poetry.
Classification: LCC PS3603.A43895 W48 2024 (print) | LCC PS3603.
A43895
   (ebook) | DDC 811/.6--dc23/eng/20240508
LC record available at https://lccn.loc.gov/2024018614
LC ebook record available at https://lccn.loc.gov/2024018615

10 9 8 7 6 5 4 3 2 1

Cover design: Paraclete Design
Cover art: Paraclete Design

Published by Paraclete Press
Brewster, Massachusetts
www.paracletepress.com

Printed in the United States of America

Contents

III. Seed Leaves / 71

I.

After
All Danger
of Frost

AN EAR TO THE GROUND

We see before we hear the thunder, and cannot
taste the rumble of tectonic plates
until too late, when stones are brought like teeth
from dead earth. On what large infinity
we live. Earth sinks into the wider
plane. A raindrop dropped into the sea.
Listen closely, with just your heels, and
you might hear the unforgotten start:
the sun that rose after days of rain,
how it made the almost cloudless sky
grow over the Shenandoah mountains;
and then more than ever feel how small
we are, and how large.

COLLECTING RAIN SAMPLES
IN A STORM

I. The Start
Robert warned me
when he saw the sudden skunk
on the roadside, *Roll*

up your window, what are you doing?
But I'd never seen one. When it lifted its tail, Robert
sped away, relieved and laughing.

And now, invincible, we climbed
a mountain in an old car
together.

II. The Storm
Then the thunder raged. The night
brightened when it was hit
by white lightning

and rain
flooded our eyes
(we were outside the car), blind,

and when we could see, lightning
flashed into trees and
Robert said, *Get your head low —*

But where
could I hide on this plateau?
Like Jonah, I knew

I was no match.
How could I not stare at the sky
which heaved itself at us, and tore the trees

down to roots?
And so we ran, and laughed, giddy
and afraid; the plateau's high grass

slowed us, our feet slipped, webs
of rain slick as sleet beneath our boots;
and we outran rain,

crouched, ducking
the lowering sky which touched the mountainside
like God;

and in this way we made it to the trees;
their soaked leaves limp
with too much water.

And there, too young,
we took the rain and left,
clothes sagging and sad

at the end, forgetting to praise
the world, its wonder
and its long-forgotten places.

TO KNOW THE EARTH BY TOUCH

The nothingness of dark first turned to light:
the earliest uncertainty. The pain
of the eclipse, the searing blindness — bright
cannot describe it. Nothing can. Contained
in light is every color. Rays that shatter
rods; waves that widen cones until
their edges are like lakes, scattering
their width as waterdrops on land, aching to spill
over the basin of the mind —
fragile and self-satisfied, that only sees
the shape. That plots a path. That finds
itself among the world's first trees
and wants too much more than peace. No; rest
at last. Lie on the Earth — on the dirt, and the dust.

WITH STARS STINGING THE SKY

The woods were like a sea, thick and loud
with green, we nearly drowned—the five of us,
at night in Catoctin's summer, camping because
here we could be this close
to the dark which was a part of everything:
seeping into the tents and between trees, and being breathed like
life in our lungs.
                    Remember the stars?
Remember how sharp-edged they were, glittering and stinging the sky
out of need like a bee. Stinging because they were alive
that night, as we were — all of us, one mass, the Earth
swirling in its black sea, radiating back against the sun,
quietly absorbed into the night which, then, was everything.

YOU ARE

the wind and its first gasp
across the sea,
too dark and not yet filled with life
you will nourish over slow
moving centuries,
will form as clay with hands and air
and with soft light, will breathe into
that we might breathe you out.

WHEN I READ ABOUT ASTEROIDS HEADED TO EARTH, I TRY TO THINK ABOUT ANYTHING ELSE

Science like a funhouse Babel —
glassbent, stretched toward the sky, our eyes
curved like planets, their great gravities
pulling sight from heaven. But who are we
when streaking meteors drift like leaves
through space and — oh — are moving toward us, spiral-
ing like angels?

HISTORY SPEAKS IN ITS DRY VOICE

Pick any thirty years. See the pain
that colors them faintly. Flat landscapes where
once buildings stood, should stand, stood when planes
as loud as thunder flattened houses. There,
my uncle lived, a Middle Eastern man
whose house
was taken and standing
in the Palestinian streets, his family without
anything, he thought, *I have to earn
it back, somehow.* He didn't. My dad
escaped and says he will never return.

***

I am American. I cannot speak
in Arabic because my father said
I would have an accent. He keeps
a part of his past on his tongue. The dead
to him still live and so
I cannot know him like I wish I could.
My dad has choked, swallowing
suffering; he has warmed it in his blood.

***

Jerusalem that stones its prophets, had
its chance and cast it away like dice.
It glows eternal, dead land, history —

how much you look like any other place
when I think of what I cannot see,
your people who do not all look alike
but do to me. I haven't seen their eyes
at home, only in unnatural light:
wide-painted with thick brushes, generalized
Arabs, poor, abused

                         and Dad says,
yes we were poor but
                    there are no
words for what we lost. and we were raised
to be strong. we are strong.

But my father's past he keeps
inside his chest. It sits there like dust,
like dead skin; or it seeps
like sores and then I get a hushed
glimpse of some richness before it fades
to the colors of the desert, a yellow
that anyone can paint: a yellow grayed
as pages of a book kept closed.

COVERED IN MOSS

These days grow slowly. Slow falling
leaves; walks with dogs; even they
seem tired. Dust floats in the still light that seeps
through the windows, and the dust
stays there, decaying in the air. Fall's spell
is here. Halloween shadows darken corners
and nothing moves much here. I miss

in bone-deep ways the words for spring —
distinct, untrackable smells and colors — flowers
which now I half-see, see blandly in my mind, half-
smell as being *sweet* and *green* and *limitless*.

The gray of today's sky is serious. Spring is far away,
invisible, cloud-shaded as a ghost.
And the days harden like ancient trees.
See the logs which sit in the grass
covering themselves in moss?

THE END OF NOVEMBER

Like they must go and are late
the leaves across the street gust, are rushing
east, I think — told like the bones of bears
when it is time, when hibernation

begins.
         The neighbors' windchimes collide, they are plates
dropped in a sink, and the wind keeps crashing
things into things, one flag tears,
its seams fraying — a sign, the neighbors say, of some great tribulation.

The season, though, somehow
                         lounges.
                                   It runs late,
the teeth of winter just barely
                         showing,
unseen, still growing somewhere under the earth. Some carry
within their bodies that clock of natural obedience.

How many weeks are left, when the light
outweighs the dark and leaves the sky glowing,
cracks it open? — bluewhite-and-graypinkgold marry,
melt, move; thin, fade in a sudden motion.

Not many, I don't think. All will be right.
Shed the summer skin, quietly hoping
for a quick winter. Sleep. And into windowpane-cracks comes air
ice cold already, and winter like grace slips in.

PRAYING FOR THE END OF THE COLD SEASON

I. Remember?

Spring glowed in the green
of leaves, rest for eyes, dulling light
like cloth, softening it.

II. Soften the Stones

The lepers had no home. Their only hope
was pity. They kept apart and waited to die.

Winter sinks around us like a shroud, its taut lines
white. Stillness coats the ground
down to small particles. Let

some new breath rattle the doors,
tear the temple cloth over and over until
its tatters float like fallen leaves away

LIFE IS / FOR THINE IS THE

One scene: The ice-hemmed trees shake rigid
gems, their limbs frozen, unblemished by cold
but stay as love does, heart-fresh, encoiled.

Another scene: The shaking half-friends who
lost a child. Their first. The cool
blue sky like ice, a wide world, hollow.

SETTLING THE STORM

Still me as you stilled the wild sea,
terror-teethed with waves cresting over
the edges of the boats, the water black like
deep-dreams, possessed by some dark thing
and screaming rain like threats. Then, call me over

that I might sink. That I can, deep-figured,
soar up toward the sky.

BEATEN AND ROBBED IN BALTIMORE, WHERE SAMARITANS ARE HARD TO FIND

She had asked, twice, that he not go tonight.
Just to see his friends. What wastefulness.
It was a premonition, she had said.
The night was full of shadows and fouled
with odd sights. His friends would still be there
tomorrow, she said. He would not be moved
by her. He would move the night.

***

Three fell on him like wolves. The flash of teeth
as bright as steel, and steel as sharp as fire.
They left him thinned of what few bills he had
left, lying in his excrement.

***

He lay in dust and dried blood and didn't see the light
on Caton Street, the people journeying, their silent
glances, afraid of the eyes
that would turn him from an icehard thing
into a man, near death. That gap is wide
as a field. *There will be some-*
one.

       To die with nothing, only
torn clothes and unmended bones;
this could not be the end.

***

Embarrassment isn't it. Nor *doubt*.
Perhaps *decorum*, or something close to shame
kept the priest apart, kept his breath
chained to his chest, in case some part of him
would meld with blooded blackness. The red eyes
were a sign. Drug abuse. What
could he do now? With his girded
heart, he moved away. On tiptoe, almost.
Looking toward the sky. Clean as air.
As light as light itself.

MARTYRS OF THE CRISTERO WAR

They've faced a wall of steel, their faces
aglow as soldiers held them
hostage, guns trained
at their hearts,

their minds
someplace
else

A SMALL SWEETNESS

This is what I need:
A small sweetness
In a cupped hand
And as soft
As bird feathers

That says in ways
Only hands can say
How beautiful this is

How this is the soul
Of life

A GLIMPSE OF BIRDS

I've seen and loved them:
the birds, the mess
of wings, the beaks
that stab, the disrespectful
looks — like feathers falling down
from my feeder. Their nectar
eyes, striped sparrows and hummingbirds all raging
shapes and the reds — endless flapping, small lives
on wires. Sound-colored. Cardinals, sometimes goldfinches
dive across
my lawn for food. Then off toward the sky.

Their words are theirs, and strange. I
imitate the sounds, but they
see through this nonsense.
Knowing the truth of things, they rise
to a world they alone can name.

ARAB MEN DON'T CRY, MY FATHER SAYS

On Google Maps, I drink them in, these names
that swim in sounds: *Ramallah, alZa'im,*
like the names of dreams. But my dad
has lived there, has felt his history tugging
at him like a leash, has visited
the Dead Sea (on the screen, a thick blue slug).
Nothing lives there, Dad says. The salinity
is ten times that of the ocean. *It is the Dead Sea.*

I cannot see what he saw.
How do I sense it? The vendors on the street,
knafeh fresh and warm, feces
walled in with burning garbage.
                          These things
exist somewhere.
                  I'm pulled toward them by sounds:
Amman and *Gaza,*
in his voice, the smile he has kept,
surviving in these places, still alive,
outliving violence. The ten-minute drive
that took two hours:
                     the checkpoint guards
held him up.
            The walls of memory come down
like rubble, splinter like a broken door,
and his eyes freeze with fear.
                    I forget

the rest, he says. *That was years before
I left.* But what of Jericho? Ofra? Efrat?
No. He's finished now. Quietly, I let
his eyes move away.

                         The sea recedes from the shore.

II.

Which Seeds Will Grow?

"Nothing we do is complete,
which is another way of saying
that the kingdom always lies beyond us."

"The Romero Prayer"

YOU ARE

the tongue twists, the stuttered
sacred *sanctus*,
the slope toward you
still too steep to tread.
We slip.
     You are the Ancient Wind,
filled with your name,
willed before the world,
which was smaller than
a palm.

     On tree-deep trails we
see only shadows.

CAN YOU HEAR HIM AT THE START?

...the light shines in the darkness,
and the darkness has not overcome it.
— John 1:5

I. Languishing Alone

I never thought I'd starve for the touch
of a stranger's elbow as I ride

a metro car so bare of passengers
I feel a part of the machine, my breath

erased in the darkened tunnels, a stranger
to myself. It is a sort of death.

We wait, who have no words for waiting. Hushed,
we long within our bones. We hide.

II. A Night of Music

When Christ is born, the angels cry aloud
                              the song that shivers through them
in waves of joy, an overwhelming cloud

of music, sound aching up toward the sky,
and raining down as starlight, as midnight cold,
as radiant faces, wings that terrify,
and messages that fulfill the oldest

of the ancient words. Here is peace at last.
Here, surrounded by old hay and crowded
so thick breath sticks in their throats, peace passes
around from hand to heart. The sound

                         impossible: A cry. A sacred hymn.

III. The Swelling Song, Together

When God created life: That first flash
in breathed words. The crashing
waves. Unshaped water. Waves. Then love
that moves as light through veins; the new
day, and then tomorrow, an eternity of
tomorrows — heaven as the first and truest union.

God forms the earth anew. Every star
born of that light, no matter how far-
flung into the dark, is a part
of its own ecosystem, a heart

that beats beneath the crust, vibrating.
Can you hear the chorus of the strings?
They flash as sun flares, blinding with their glow,
aiming outward, curving back towards home,

and how the noise returns me to the start:

a voice I loved when I was young; back then,

the thread of gold: first light; creation marked

for you; the speck-thin spear, still lodged within

my heart; the brilliance of creation. I still

catch a glimpse of it sometimes: when once
I watched a star streak through the dark, the thrill
of something sacred happening; or when
I fail to love, leave, return again;
or when I'm blinded by the sinking sun.

UNSPEAKING

At times, we move away from words, letting
looks speak: the sweep that leaves suggestions
like crumbs. Sometimes, these are pushed

toward the pain of unsaid things. Then
they are like stones, or like teeth, already
crumbling against themselves.

                When you return,
the sweetness too cannot be hardened into words,
but melts like sweet cheese *knafeh*, warm dough
that yellows toward brown, tasting only like honey.

THE LANGUAGE LOST AT EDEN

The garden ground is colored by our blood.
We cannot tongue out the sound of leaves
leaking life like a red wound. Trees
named *malum punicum*, named something like
sin, are seen unspoken,

                         spokes of broken light spike
through holes in foliage.

                              We wear these leaves as skin.
We wade through mud.
We feel life pawing at our veins, and
drying like a creature in the sun.

THE PEACE THAT HIDES

Still, *Shantih* haunts me in my sleep.
Like the afterlife — clichéd in golden light,
or else a sentence kept somewhere — the deep
of truth like matter, in shapes that we can't know.

I rest in that uncertainty sometimes,
almost passing out, waking right
before I see past the veil, the lines
just starting to *mean*, the early glow
of morning. To know the maker's heart — that
would be something. But it wouldn't be
peace. Just knowledge, that long-forgotten Tree,
deep-rooted in my want. The broken back
that labor curved, and the human need for rest:
It noses at me like
some tired thing; it curls within my chest,
or else I feel the first sharp stings of its bite —

and I am no more found than when we were cast
out of the garden, guilty, staring back
and seeing the fires glowing like light at last.

SPARKS

For Aaron C.

Your first cry burst life apart,
and there you were — chaos, doctors, noises
gone; you: too large to hold inside
my heart; to small to bear weight: the pain
of age, of loss, mistakes that crash
into each other leaving dust and
glass words I will not let myself think
out loud.

        When you've grown, you will
see. You are new: as strange as light
that bends around a planet, shaped
around itself. See how it still warms?
See how it becomes its own shape?

PERFORMING FOR NO ONE BUT THEMSELVES

I watch them when they're playing or engaged
in thought — the shriek, the look of wonder. It's only then
I get a real glimpse: the open page
of a face, eyes as bright
as my wife's, the echoes
of cells somehow combined
to make life. But it grows

away from us. The gardener's burden. Plants
shed their seeds.
Freedom to flowers — to sit and watch their wildness
spread.

PRAYERS FOR A SAFE TRIP

For Jed C.

These prayers smoke-float from my lips, *full*
of grace, the Lord is with thee. Words
that tint the air, warming me as I drive
home. And I breathe them in   and out:
watching snow fall
like stars, watching snow dust the asphalt;
brightening the night as it drifts,

but watching too as it starts to slick the lines of lanes
soaked on the street; it grows deeper; thickens to sleet,
quickeningly falls, when it is white and blinding,
falling and falling I remember suddenly slipping,

spinning, moving at nightmare-speed toward the guard rail, wheels
gripping
nothing in the snow, and all around I see
the flakes like glowing lights, like stars,
like wild smoke, and
I hear my own voice, screaming
a prayer without faith
but with need,
and dizzy at the white specks swirling
against the nightglass windows
I am half blind but know only
that I will die and
can do nothing
but pray

PIERCING THE LEAVES

See through Adam's hiding place
among the leaves, his secret sin blooming
like a flower, red-shading his face.
He tucks his sin within himself: a wound
rooted deeper than trees. He named
them *ash* because the Lord lent him a small look
at language. And now his shame

sits on his animal tongue, holds it like a hook,
and he is afraid and small. He knows
how much he lost, sees it slip away
and knows that *she* must know, wants to show her
all is not gone; but the way
she will not look at him is enough.
And so he sees it through, these long days,
this life too much
to bear alone. And he waits,
embarrassed, too afraid even to touch
her with his thoughts, too afraid to hope, to ask
for anything. He has taken on so much
already. He tries not to think of the past.

THE LOVE THAT USED TO MOVE ME

most mornings, love would pull at me, would put
its hands inside my hands and pull me up,
would animate my feet, make air of my smile.

I am older now by many years.
I sit and eat and think. I sleep.
I think I will sleep all winter.

what words are said in the silence
of a look? in the shadow of
movement? leaning on a wall for shape,
leaving only what they were behind —
only breath that spreads through open spaces
like a spill.

ON PRAYER

It takes the heart and cracks it in half:
Like lightning striking a dead tree, fire grows
from the wood, blossoms a red flower until living
grass withers
                    in the heat,
heat that swallows air as water,
eats the earth and burns
and burning everything
grows until its death is an impossibility

until it dies. And the ground is richer for it.

ST. PETER SWALLOWS KIERKEGAARDIAN UN-TRUTHS

Then Peter said to him in reply,
"Explain this parable to us."
      — *Matthew 15:15*

Peter's ears are stinging with these stories:
seeds and penitents, usuries
praised. There is pain enough.
Their brains smash shut, and his ears
are already mostly closed.

                If instead
He'd turn back to those large signs, tear in two
the sin-hearted skeptics, pour from them praise as drink,
raise the dead again, back when no one
questioned Him — if He'd jab into their righteousness
His thumb, then Peter could abide it. But not

now. What eats at him? Everything
he left at the feet of this man.
He understands only this: he can't
know anything.

          So he forces shut his eyes,
foresees himself as one can see the coming of a storm, sees himself

one day dragged behind an imperially white
horse and squints, sees behind him in
the dust a broken trail of his browning blood;

and he sits silented — knows this vision hails
some portent he'll never understand.

THE THINGS WE LEAVE UNSAID

Your eyes speak in languages I know
are mysteries. The way your joy grows
like a flower, stretching like a slow

morning. It moves deliberately towards delight.
It simmers. It sits there like a campfire,
tired from the stories, smiling.

Stay
for just a second. How many days
are left to us?

OTHERS, OURS

"Parents of 545 Children Separated
at the Border Cannot Be Found"
— The New York Times

In night's blanket-blackness, my daughter
screams and beats her bed, her head a weight
still sunk in nightmare. She tries to ask —
where's Mom? before her voice breaks.
She is two. She bursts with hurt and I wonder
if she sees what I cannot:

                                        we

hadn't said *detainment* but last night
I said *abuse* and
like if someone took our girl or maybe even
Lily. It hovers like a shadow over my head.

SMALLING VOICES

You cannot silence all of us at once.
We live and stain like blood.

You   silence   us   once.
We live   like blood.

You   silence   us
                     like blood.

You   us
                     blood.

You

TRYING TO UNDERSTAND LOVE

The thick humidity is weighted and I
pray for peace, but I know I'm really just
praying for rain: rain to burst the sky
in two, turn violent blue to black, turn crust-
hard earth to mud again — the world post-flood.
Heat-death. It gathers like a storm
that will not break, is beating in my blood,
growing like cancer as it warms.

How can I pray
for anyone on days like this?
And then my daughter slips and falls, her arms splay
like a rude cross and I kiss
her knee. A cloud cools the air with shade,
and I see how the world was first made.

NEARING THE END OF BRIGHT THINGS

It shows up out of nowhere gusting in
like breath, like life, erasing yesterday
and days before — I'll ask again, just stay.

Just for another minute when our words
will almost touch,
                    before side-stepping us,
growing thinner in the open air, and
floating off without saying goodbye

FORGETTING EVERYTHING WE'VE KILLED

We cannot speak about the fear:
wherever we rest we will die. Keep
peace. Speak to no one.
Shut your eyes to the sun.
Survive, and eat the world and the easy meals and
savor and soften, and softly fall asleep.

I'm desperate for a sign we cannot miss:
some pillar, rising in fire, that twists
itself toward heaven, screaming out flames
like scared birds and promising a clean, whole land: a home
if we would still ourselves —
sit like stones and listen to the earth,
the felt noise that runs beneath the dust,
buried with our first names.

TRYING TO EXPLAIN WHAT *KNAFEH* IS

now a country away from the old
land, we mispronounce food we no longer
eat. *make it here,* you said,
find whatever you want
there is everything

no. we are still looking for *waraq da'wali's*
soft skin, finding in kind-meant compliments
that bitterness — *how delicious! so this is made*
of cheese?

       well technically yes but
    not   American cheese

    it is named   sweet cheese

which is strange. it is even strange
to me — what makes
it sweet? sweet cream? they have that
here. in arabic, *bu'aza,* which we

cannot hear without hearing dad's joke — that
sugar-and-ice-cream is *sukur w bu'aza*
but to a child it was *sakhal bu'zik,* which he told
to the shopkeeper and which means
shut your mouth.

only now google

translates it as *asimat*

which is a word we do not know.

what sounds like

kataifi? nothing we can make

here. nothing I have ever tasted before.

THE ALTAR FLOWERS BOWED LIKE SAINTS

Yesterday the altar flowers lowered their heads like saints,
like they needed rain, barely
alive.
    And today they are gone,
tossed like chaff in the trash
or moved to a parishioner's house
to wait on some pale windowsill
until forgetfulness kills it
or it dies from some other neglect.

SIMULACRUM OF LIFE

I. Two Miracles
How thin it is, the Host, held
in a monstrance, softskin, so light
light moves through it. It is a screen that hides
breath.

At best, it is the narrow path.

II. Healing the Blind
My eyes are grayed; sin-thickened and closed,
                                           log-heavy; and
my prayer is old and tired and poor,
rote and long-inhabited.

                               What happens when
the monstrance's light reflects?
First, newness — curves, bending the room,
blending the windows with the light and
the light plays
tricks, looks
alive, flickers the way
candled-gold moves, how
the fire, blue-seated
bleeds into the gold, the white tip stinging
like a coast-broken sky.
It looks like the sea at morning.
It shatters my sight.

RESTING IN THE PAST

For Mitchell

The lightning flash of life is gone
before the sound of it rumbled out
and shook the ground like rocks rolled from tombs,
upending the natural order — clattering
through the family, tearing us like cloth,
pulling from us sounds that have their own matter
now — silent prayers. Sobs shatter
them apart.

        It is deeper than the words
we speak at the funeral.
                The memory,
that's all. And pictures. And tomorrow

impossibly large, a thousand
unspeakable stories, black as thunder clouds.

For now I'll just stay here
in the church, praying,
trying not to see my aunt in tears.
I'll stay here, eyes closed,
sleeping, praying, resting in the past.

NOAH, PROUD AND REACHING FOR THE FORM OF GOD

So as not to be thought of as a fool,
he laid his plans and prayed the math would work

a miracle. That somehow all these sticks
would keep the animals and crew afloat,
beyond one weight.

                        He also prayed for rain. For so much it
would blind everything. The rings

philosophers had claimed to see in space,
these were the things he drew upon. Angels; swords

of light. He knew by heart endless death.
What will die so we can live?

He gives himself to auguries — sees in the shape
of birds some burning world, flames like waves.

But he prays to outlive them all.
Fall rain like falling stars. Spare me.

He is not a perfect man; he will sin.
What can he do but build? This act

is all he knows — he builds like an ant.
He can't see past the lumber or the crew.

As harrowing as life is, this is worse.
To live (*how long?*) within the hands of God.

What did he know of that?

SCARS AND STILLNESS

Our tree was lightning-struck, a burned scar
where its branches grew. And I knew
this disappointing thing, death, loomed larger
than it should — just black-ashed wood and leaf. How few
sadnesses remain. This one
somehow did. I couldn't shake the memory —
the dark edges, teethed like jagged bones,
the deadened black wood, the fresh-lost green,
like Golgotha, somehow — the lifelessness of stone.

I look across the yard, cross it
looking for vague comforts, some mound
of life, some true movement: birds, a line of sun-
light so alive with hope it buzzes with sound;
nothing. I rest here, sunk
in silence that sweeps into new air —
the stillness moving toward me like a prayer.

THE VIOLENCE OF THE WORLD'S FIRST SONGS

Where are the raging waves you threw
to the shore at its birth? Or the wild water before
Christ came to calm the sea? I can hear you
in my past as storms that shook the floor.

The shaking reverence for the golden Ark
that killed, for the world of wind and breath
that wrecked the land as storms do? Beneath

the chapel's silence, I have the noises past:
The crack of creation, when you split the dark
into a thousand things, each shining. The crash
of the waves upon the shore, the first sea.
The silence calls out for the absent thunder,
when once the world roared wildly,
and rumbled, full of noise and ancient wonder.

VINES, BRANCHES

Anyone who does not remain in me
will be thrown out like a branch and wither.
  — John 15:6

The cool air lung-filled
with the thin breath of fall.
There, across the walking path a leaning tree —

a charred, black-toothed wreck lightning had killed
years ago while around it green trees stood tall.
Leaning numbly

against nothing, the ivy-greened branches tilted
it toward the greener trees, and all
its vines crept across its limbs, their green

a new coat, a new protocol
for life: that the green
of life could give those still

limbs the movement of a dance, the lilting
sway of leaves; it was a morality play scene,
this absurd dead tree standing against the fall.

LOST ON A HIKE WITH MY FAMILY

here
when it grows dark
and you are lost
in thoughts
of death
you pretend
to know the way through this incredible green
because
to say anything else
would be to lose them all already;
and you pray without words
and almost without hope

until Teta Denise springs like
history, that strange flower
inside your blood,
and you see her Jerusalem
and the houses taken,
gripping in her fists like teeth the pain
and poverty and death —

and you hear her,
a sternness that scared you,
hushing you, firmly
taking you into her arms — now
and when you broke
into her garden
to smell the rough stems
of her tomato plants —

and you freeze
and you listen
as she sings
in the old language
songs that still
the world.

GRATITUDE

As you mow the lawn again this month,
and mind the rows, not straight, but at least not
a mess? and as you swat at flies
and pray no screaming yellowjackets come

(even their sound sounds like a heart-stabbing fire),
pray you'll stay unstung, unbitten, unburned —
and squash down the Sisyphean thought
that all is for nothing. *Think*: this is

a sort of murder. Or if *murder* is
too bloated, too full of hate,
then this is still a barren field of pride.
At your most dramatic, think, *I'll die*

of melanoma. Or think, *A barren field*
of pride. Curse Adam. Or curse homeownership.
Curse the ground. *Thorns and thistles*
it shall bear for you. For you are dust

and aching for an ancient sort of rain —
as large as heaven, heavy as God's voice.
No rain comes, of course. Not today.
But after it is done, at least for one

sweet hour, hear how all the birds
come calling, a chirping noise to sing
of the world-feast, a chorus giving
thanks for what they are provided.

PRAYING THE SORROWFUL MYSTERIES
IN SPRING

But in this new brightness, the crown
of thorns is made of spikes of light
shining through tree leaves, scattering
the light   shattered on the ground,   like
silver pieces of white fire shining,
cracking into lines;
then the warmth and everywhere
is a new world already —
that breathes   so loudly
its gusts shake the trees
to their roots; and shake the rose
petals from their stems
until the floor is streaked
with all these spilled
pinks and reds and whites.

THE MOWING THAT WOKE MY DAUGHTER

They are not my enemy
I remind myself,
though they are
tearing up the public hill just past my fence
with loud tools and
hacking with weed whackers the wild violets
and new lavender spread
across the hill in bird patterns.
We had watched them grow.

One worker paused
at the flare of yellow tulips, and I saw him
from my window look
around for a second, and
leave them, then look around and
separate the small flowers
from their stems, half-
pausing to step over them with his boot,
leaving to finish his job.

When they move to farther hills
I will see it from the right perspective —
as a small, inevitable injury.
I know this. But here, at home, I am left
with the broken yellow-purple bruising and the memories
of my father: who saw
Israeli jets swoop over his house in Jerusalem and a

military helicopter fire finger-length bullets
into the hill in his front yard
and I wonder what seeds will grow from this,
what next year will look like, and what sort of
hate it is to watch things fall apart.

III.

Seed Leaves

"Remember when you were little,
you composed lines of awe;
you collected epiphanies."

Ewa Chrusciel, "A Poet and a Shrink (III)"

SINGING INTO BEING

First you sang the note of our creation,
drawing from the deepest void the root
of truth. With words the first delineation:
Light, and dark. The un-thundered sky mute.
The patient stripe of lightning in the eye
of the mind, silent as a thought.
Breath, thick with the need to be,
to make a solidness from what is not;
thick with song, with man and life and sea,
with unthought animals and land and sky:
and still it carries, like seeds, ancient words,
a world that echoes in vibrating chords,
a command and a promise: says, *arise*

YOU ARE

You are the first breath at dawn,
the yawned exhale,
whale-deep air and blue,
who swallowed man and
resurrected him, who chants
a prayer stretching over
the world like song —
the plucked string in endless echo
that hums the birth of time,
the uncried infancy of new light
and look,
today, how we are given
wind from the sea,
wind that rests
and moves and moves back
toward the sea,
and carries with it voice
and has a voice itself.

SOMETHING STURDIER THAN STONE

These sudden flakes fall like feathers, poured
out, glittering from the sky, swept across
the street, scattering like wild children, unmoored
from gravity, wind-shuffled, turning and tossed.
The midday sky is streaked with gray like steel.
My kids prefer to stay indoors
where it is safe. No wind to peel
away the skin with its rough tongue, or roar
through bare trees. *Hibernate with me*
while you are small enough to want to stay.
Do you see
how quickly all of this will pass? Today

is backspun, gone — whitened by
the world which spins
like some wild thing. Clouds crash in the sky,
tumble toward each other. In
my ears — the last thing: the past
still calling, the memories of the year before,
the thousand faces we have seen played. Cast
time into stone — into something sturdier
than stone. Place it in my blood, adrift
in veins, a fast-flowing stream, remembered rain-
water rushing like a flood over a cliff,
in deference to memories going on their way.

PRAYING FOR GRACE

I cannot see. I am again drowning
in the sea I nearly died in when I
was 17, while a hurricane churns
the water around me, turns me over,
fills my lungs. *I say unto you: I nearly died.*
Then and now, I thin like stones
on sand. I think I see a glimpse of God
before the sea swallows me, swallows everything,
already licking the land it birthed
at the start, returning only bones.

COME BACK FROM THE DEAD

It is Easter now, and so for forty days
at least Teta Denise can put
to sleep those worries of our deaths, the blades
of loneliness; or she can pray to quiet them. What

wonder — uncertainty, too — when
the women came and nothing was inside the cave
but air, and outside, two gleaming men
brought with them the day.

And this new joy will not be shut
in,
    leaps like fenced dogs, will not rest, it is loud and echoing
spring light — stone-shattering, shouting
newness. The wind will not rest too, spreading like roots
beneath damp ground, soaking in life, seeping
life into its veins, spreading seeds that grow like truth —
too thick to shake, remade like
Lazarus's rise from all that sleep.

RETIRING FROM TEACHING

She glazes over at once, is very close
to sleep; she will
soon; but first
she keeps bringing up
to her children
one day when she knew

enough to teach;
how she was kept
in the auditorium,
penned at an endless lecture for more than two hours,
crowded on all sides by the words
fed loudly to her by the microphonedman

as her students starved in their homes,
or cried at their small failures
which were their lives
and which she better than anyone knew

STAYING BEHIND: THE PARABLE OF THE OLDER SON

The dustclouds around him looked huge, obscene
marks against the sky. His head was hung
like an animal's. His walk was slow. It seemed
as though he didn't want to come — that it stung
past words that he was headed home. Was this home?
How? When he had taken all
his earnings from this house, when he had roamed
around, a beast, had he now the gall

to come back? No. I stayed. I had to.
Our father, broken, with simple, love-blind eyes
somehow cannot see the long game.
Justice is meted; mercy unglued
if it means open arms to any broken name
that wanders back here.

I hope he dies.

RIVER GLASS: A BAPTISM

The river's shore is covered in filth: the normal
garbage, beer cans, wrappers, even a spare
tire, some lost shoes. And four pizza boxes,
left by a group I see leave, squatting square
on the rocks, the trashcan overflowing
with more trash. The shore is false
and falling: the sky
shies back in clouds, the air buzzes with flies.

Rimmed by this mess, my kids splash in the water.

There, my daughter sees a speck of blue
between two rocks: a real blue, browned
a bit by mud and time; but shining through it
is a strange and broken light. She scans the ground
and finds more: aquas, air-thin whites,
caramels — the sun moving in them like
a breath and I hand-rinse her glass in the scented water.
The grime comes off. I'm holding only its light.

FIRST SPRING

Greens and blues, the yellow light turns red
spreading itself across the floor of the chapel,
and warms through the window. Winter ended
only yesterday; I cannot yet tell
myself, *this is it*, unprepared
to see what I already see: that man
is made of dust. Moses dared
to look into the face of God. He demanded
to know God's unpronounceable name. But
who could speak
the largeness of the Lord? — who stilled flood
waters with a word, whose thoughts could creak
to life the stone-still world? What mouth could
shape itself to that unending shape,
hold in it bread as life, as man, as blood? —
it falls on me like dust, the broken light, great
shadows, the light that blinds.

A DIFFERENT AIR

The clouds sit like kings
at the crown of the world.
Oxygen pearls into fine mist.

A miracle, outside
my desire to know,

and everywhere, God,
how yellowgreen weeds continue
and purpling wilds along both sides of Interstate 95,
overcrowded, yelling out their
colors, aching and stretching to grow.

UNKNOWABLE AS BIRDSONGS

I. Birdshapes
the cloud of sparrows like

a sea
       they follow math

I cannot voice
          or know

II. War
in the yard, one spot
of sun over which the starlings
fight

III. At the Park
we healed one goldfinch
by giving him space and warding off
curious kids
         before we left
another yellow bird came to us, stopped
on the sidewalk and chirped with so much noise
it was gratitude   that was like joy

WILDLY NEW

Everything he touched was sanctified:
the river where he chose his own baptism;
each sandcrushed footstep timeswept but
somewhere, grains transfigured by the light
still move in sacred shapes, are windblown across
the world. We, meanwhile, bear on our backs

old words we mispronounce: Eden's trees
sterilized in lines that we make straight,
packed in earth that we imagine brown,
the ooze of juice, foot-flattened fruit
that melts into the mud, and disappears;
and when we're gone grows wildly new.

MISTAKES WE MADE

I. Morning
The scattershot of light, new blindness
of morning. My eyes adjust to the sun,
to the one sound
of your voice, a cry of need
and I don't think *what about Mom*
but *how can I give you love*
that stretches past my arms
and can't be one thing
but is everything,
whatever love is,
this is
love

II. Evening
The interminable hours
when I am a shattered
glass on the floor
of our house, downed
like a tree-fallen powerline, my cup struck
from the counter,
covering you
in scalding tea
that, falling, must have
glittered like rain
    against
    your skin

SMALL COMFORTS

At night when you are asleep
already
      (on to deeper planes)
I sometimes hold your hand
so you
      aren't alone, and so
you don't go drifting off
completely. You stir, and
it is enough to know
you are there.

IN A PICTURE, A DOG HOLDS A PINK FLOWER IN ITS MOUTH

It must taste pink — even
without our complexities
of flavor, look with what
pride he lives, being only
himself, being only in love
with himself.

JUST BEYOND OUR SIGHT

Earth moves — shifting plates over sliding lines
of magma, the ebb and flow of time, the planet
gliding on dark matter, twirling, flying
through the blackness of cold space. *how can it
move through matter?* It moves through matter.
We will not ask how. But in wondering,
it's clear: when the noise of sight is shut,
we hear it, we feel the lightning thundering.

HOW TO HOLD THE TELESCOPE

For Ann T.

The narrow end could pierce skin.

                                 In spidered constellations

are pockets of dark matter — invisible, heavier than anything

on Earth. If we cannot see them,

what's the harm in looking instead

at the sun, set safely into its own pocket?

Or at the millions of new suns

being born inside the *Pillars of Creation?*

Those words alone

shift the inner sands and send me spiraling

toward God. Have you seen it?

Mountains of galaxies claw toward freedom,

reaching at once toward everywhere —

                                       their light

already mostly dead. Lightyears

tall, and we are dying:

we scale them in our minds, galaxies

away. We only see them as they

once were. Out there are truths

falling apart as they move through time,

and out there too is God,

his awe and power somewhere

farther than I can see.

                           We have his echoes, though,

but these are hard to hear.

SCORPION STINGS

He nears the end. My grandfather. He fell
at work, hit his head on a table. I
am eight or nine, just learning how to cry
and so I watch the adults. My dad can't tell
I'm feeling early tremors. He's trying to quell
his own storms. *Arab men don't cry,*
he said before. *Not even when Samir died*
from a sting and so, not now. The smell

of almost-death fills the bedroom like a cloud.

He used to beat my father. My dad
                              refused
to hit us, channeling his anger into loud
outbursts, a fist through a wall. He used
to yell, too. And now he stands
rocking, shaking, staring at his hands.

PLANTING A GARDEN

Stealing clippings from neighbors' yards
And smiling as they grew their own blooms
In the safe and hidden rooms where we
Keep watch on them like they are our children.

***

Nothing grew. We knew this was
A possibility, had read
It sometimes takes two years,
And we hoped in spite of only dirt
For the green that could be anything.

Perhaps we dug too shallow or too close
To the shade, or stepped where we had already planted,
Either crushing roots or breaking their curled
First shoots before they broke the surface.

***

So when one survived, wove a green line
Of its own, thinly sprouting something unknowable, I ran
Inside and for a moment felt
What John must have felt
Leaving Peter, old and unsteadily running,
And running breathlessly
To tell everyone —

Everyone

What had happened

And how you wouldn't believe your eyes.

ACKNOWLEDGMENTS

I'm grateful to the following journals for publishing versions of poems in this collection:

Antiphons, "Can You Hear Him at the Start?" (2021)

Capsule, "An Ear to the Ground" (2021), "The End of November," "Something Sturdier Than Stone," and "The Love That Used to Move Me" (2022)

Claw and Blossom, "A Glimpse of Birds" (2021)

Convivium, "The Violence of the World's First Songs" (2020), "The Peace That Hides" (2021)

the other side of hope, "History Speaks in Its Dry Voice," "Arab Men Don't Cry, My Father Says," and "Scorpion Stings" (2021)

Presence, "Settling the Storm" (2022)

St. Katherine's Review, "First Spring" (2021)

Vermillion, "Life Is / For Thine Is The" and "River Glass: A Baptism" (2021), "Lost on a Hike with My Family" and "Scars and Stillness" (as "A Burned Scar") (2022)

Zócalo Poetry Prize Honorable Mention, "Trying to Explain What *Knafeh* Is" (2023)

I'm grateful to all those at Paraclete Press: Lillian Miao for her reorganization suggestions, Robert Edmonson for his keen eye in spotting errors and offering thoughtful, subtle correction, Michelle Rich for accommodatingly refining the layout of the book, Olivia Tingley for her endless help and support and everything she did to get this book out in the world, and all those at Paraclete who helped in so many countless ways. Special thanks to Jessica Schnepp, who has encouraged my poetry at every opportunity and found new and unexpected avenues for it.

I want to thank my colleagues and friends who inspire me through their teaching and conversation: Kendall Black, Angie Bentzley, Kristin Dove, Andrew Graney, Jackie Hondrum, Stephen Kain, Kate Mach, John McCaul, Jessica Porter, Kari Rea, Faith Thompson, Michele Stumpf, Carol Sullivan, Lisa Troshinsky, Kathy W-B, Andy Witte, Ronnie Yates, and especially Robert Medoff for uplifting those around him and always championing his friends.

In thanksgiving for the gift of my family: Mary and Jack Calis, Anthony and Natalie Calis, Amanda and John Hale, Alex and Kathy Calis, Melissa and Rom Mascetti, Luke Atkinson, Edward and Maile Atkinson, and Fr. Patrick Mullan. And in great thanks to my incredible friends, Jacob and Ashley King and Tony and Kerry St. Leger.

Finally, a huge thanks to my wife, Stephanie, for her constant, unfailing love and encouragement, and to my children for their goodness, love for others, and sensitivity to the world around them. You are truly the greatest joys in my life.

ABOUT PARACLETE PRESS

PARACLETE PRESS is the publishing arm of the Cape Cod Benedictine community, the Community of Jesus. Presenting a full expression of Christian belief and practice, we reflect the ecumenical charism of the Community and its dedication to sacred music, the fine arts, and the written word.

SCAN
TO
READ
MORE

www.paracletepress.com

O that my words were written down!
O that they were inscribed in a book!
O that with an iron pen and with lead
they were engraved on a rock forever!

—JOB 19:23–24

IRON PEN

Outcast and utterly alone, Job pours out his anguish to his Maker. From the depths of his pain, he reveals a trust in God's goodness that is stronger than his despair, giving humanity some of the most beautiful and poetic verses of all time. Paraclete's Iron Pen imprint is inspired by this spirit of unvarnished honesty and tenacious hope.

YOU MAY ALSO BE INTERESTED IN...

www.paracletepress.com